All Roads Go Where They Will

All Roads Go Where They Will

Poems by Phyllis Beck Katz

For Steffie -
May all your roads
go where you will.
All the best,
Phyllis
3/2/14

Antrim House
Simsbury, Connecticut

Library of Congress Control Number: 2010939089

ISBN: 978-0-9843418-8-7

Printed & bound by United Graphics, Inc.

First Edition, 2010

Front cover painting: "High Road" by Edward Hopper
© Heirs of Josephine N. Hopper,
licensed by the Whitney Museum of American Art

Author photograph by Ellen Augarten

Book design by Rennie McQuilkin

Antrim House
860.217.0023
AntrimHouse@comcast.net
www.AntrimHouseBooks.com
21 Goodrich Road, Simsbury, CT 06070

To Arnie: for our 51 years

...we are together still
this Nankang morning;
discovery does not matter.
Time's feathers hold their breath for us.
Hope is just a leaf,
a branch away.

Acknowledgements

The following publications first presented poems appearing in this volume, often in earlier versions:

Bloodroot Literary Magazine: "At the Bridge," "Losing"
The Breath of Parted Lips, II: "Tears of Horses"
Connecticut River Review: "Winter"
Cooking on the Wild Side: "Berries on the Tongue," "Winter Soup"
Ekphrasis: "Painting the Night"
New England Anthology: "Night Train," "Remnants"
The Salon: "On the Train to Cambridge"
Still Puddle Poets: "Ode to the Ephemeral," "Through Windows," "The Day You Came Back," "The Placemat"
Still Puddle Poets – New Poems: "Beacon Wood," "Now the Fall," "Raven Call"

"Winter Wren" received First Prize in the Alumni Hall and Ammonoosuc Region Arts Council Poetry Contest, 2009.

Thanks to the Whitney Museum of American Art for permission to reproduce Edward Hopper's "High Road."

I am indebted to the late Donald Sheehan, former Director of the Frost Place in Franconia, N.H. with whom I had the privilege and joy of teaching poetry at Dartmouth, and to Cynthia Huntington, April Ossmann, Pamela Harrison, Maxine Kumin, B.H. Fairchild, Vijay Seshadri and Henri Cole, whose workshops have helped to shape my poetry. My thanks also to the members of my poetry group, Still Puddle Poets, for our many years of working together.

All Roads Go Where They Will, my first book, is composed of early and recent poems, both published and unpublished. I am fortunate and grateful that the skilled hands and wisdom of poet and editor Rennie McQuilkin have guided its production and brought it to fruition.

Table of Contents

And it was at that age... Poetry arrived
in search of me. I don't know, I don't know where
it came from, from winter or a river.
I don't know how or when,
no, they were not voices, they were not
words, nor silence,
but from a street I was summoned,
from the branches of night,
abruptly from the others,
among violent fires
or returning alone,
there I was without a face
and it touched me.

Pablo Neruda, "Poetry"

Prelude

Two Self-Portraits after Magritte

You ask: "Paint me who you are, but use my brush."

1. Recusatio

I am sitting with my back to you
on an upright chair floating in mid-air on a blue canvas.
To my right, above my shoulder, a locked book,
its shape — an artist's palette
splashed with word colors:
pudenda, Anti-Christ, franks and beans.
(If I must use these colors,
I cannot paint a portrait
for you that is mine. I have no key
for this book.)

2. Adfirmatio

I'm still floating on the chair
and there's another book, locked too,
but colored by another palette —
words I've found along the paths I've walked:
solitude, anthem, palinode, dome, berries.
The key lies in the reading —
you only need to use a wider lens.
Come to my cellar (if you'll permit
a metaphor aged by Horace).
Drink deeply of my wine:
you may find it mature.

I. Generations

The generations of mankind are as leaves.
The autumn wind shakes them to the ground,
but the forest blooms with life once more
as spring comes round again. So we are born
and grow, and so we pass away.

Homer, *Iliad VI,* 146-149
(translation by the author)

Choices

She held her life in her own hands
as if it were a robin's egg
just fallen from a nest,
its fragile surface yet uncracked,
life within it
waiting
like an unsung song.

She held her life in her warm palms,
touched its shell with shaking fingers
and felt the warmth inside —
beak and claws and feathers
still unborn.

She held her life in her own hands,
green-blue ovum of possibility —
forked tail or angel's wing.

In her own hands
it was her life she held.
She was afraid
and she was glad.

Dream Kitchen

I walked across the old, familiar tiles
of red, and green and yellow,
each faded by much scrubbing
and sectioned off with thick black lines
providing structure and a kind of order
often absent from the household where they lay.
It was a realm where peace and happiness
were residents, but often not at home.
And as I walked, I tried to call them back.

I found the worn spot by the sink,
burned place by the stove,
square with faintly carved initials
inscribed once by a brother
armed with a birthday jackknife,
a young epigrapher who dared
to leave his sign and was, of course,
found out and made to pay.

I visited each corner of the room,
ice box, pantry, closet for the brooms,
entries to the breakfast room and porch,
window broken in a hurricane,
door that opened to the cellar,
tiny lavatory just beyond
where I would hide from other kinds of storms
too often raging within our house.

Gone were the smells of baking,
roasting, frying, sautéing, broiling,
gone the steady flow of water, clash of pots and pans,
scrape of plates, hiss of roiling steam.
Vanished the choruses of chopping, peeling, dicing,
cacophonic promises of every preparation.

But I could hear the songs and sudden laughter,
sense the all-too-often hidden tears,
the joys and sorrows of this one domain,
place where my mother should have been a queen.

Sundays, Ocean Grove, N.J. 1945

The town was still on Sundays, no cars along the streets,
no radio stations playing, no children's voices sweet.
The chairs on rows of stern front porches did not dare to rock;
it was as if the town were closed and barred by chain and lock.
The only sounds were organ peals, the endless hymns that rose
from the Great Auditorium, heart of church-born Ocean Grove.
Within the dark and narrow house, my grandparents' last home,
I tired of my favorite books, longed for sand and ocean's foam,
found no comfort in the pungent roasts, our Sunday fare,
detested the odor of the smelling salts that always filled the air
to help my grandmother endure the desperate gasps for breath
of my grandfather's last summer, his slow and painful death.
On those endless summer Sundays, I often fled their grief
to hide beneath the boardwalk on the day's forbidden beach.

Birth of an Agnostic

I thought nothing awful ever happened
in my small town. Well, if it did,
my parents kept it quiet. Behind closed doors
they listened to the radio. They hid the newspapers.
Protected in an endless infancy, I knew
we had gone to war somewhere far across the ocean.
I saw blue and gold stars in front windows.
I helped knit washcloths for the soldiers overseas,
collected pennies to buy a corn cob pipe
for General MacArthur.

Crocheted doilies protected the comfy sofa
of my mind. But in 1945 I saw the photographs in *Life*.
A classmate had smuggled the magazine
to school and circulated it on the playground.
Those lines of starving prisoners
along the barbed wire, crematorium chimneys,
piles on piles of naked, skeletal remains —
beginnings of a life of doubt.

Sixteen

She stood in the middle of the babies' section
hating it all — the early getting up, the bus ride
into town, the older salesladies who lorded
over her, the endless refolding and tidying
little shirts, tiny socks, blankets, and diapers.
There was the phone to answer, customers to serve,
and always, always, admonitions — she "was too young,"
she "had to learn, she "didn't get it right again,"
she "wouldn't last." She hated going home
to help with meals and do the dishes, hated
being tired, despised the waiting for another day to come,
another bus ride to the hot and sticky town.

When she could, she retreated to the stockroom
to tie up parcels and label them for shipping.
She loved the solitude, the single light bulb
casting shadows in curious shapes
upon the wall, loved the cool, the looming towers
of empty boxes, all sorted out by sizes, like children
lining up for school, the smell of ink and paste,
coarseness of the coils of twine between her fingers,
the giant plastic cans, plump with bags of trash
like well-fed matrons, arms filled with purchases.
Sometimes while she was working there
Mike, the store's old janitor came by.
Most of all she loved to talk to him.

Mike brought the mail and took away the trash,
and there was little time for conversation,
but she found out that in the dimness of his past,
he had sailed on a merchant ship,
crossed oceans to places with exotic names,
and when he spoke of traveling open seas to Bali or Japan,
in the dark quiet of the stockroom, she could hear the waves,
could smell the water, feel the breath of ocean breezes
in her hair — a ship, heading out.

Night Train

Waiting for the night train in a woods in rural Maine,
a girl, alone, your knapsack packed with books and hope,
you stand upon a platform etched by iron tracks,
by loneliness and darkness and the falling snow.
Amidst the empty woods there is no station
to offer warmth from cold that chills the stars
and makes the moon retreat into the clouds;
there is no shelter from the ice-tongued wind
that licks its frosty breath against your cheeks
in silence, for the snow has covered every sound.

You are alone, and yet you do not mind
the growing cold, or fear the separation
from family ties and comfort of your home.
You seem to gain a strength in isolation,
and, yes, the night train when it comes
confirms it all — its light that slowly grows
inside the dark is gleaming just for you;
the humming of the rails, the echo in the ancient
wooden planks that shape the platform,
the squeal of slowing wheels sing out to you
and call you to a journey through the night.

It is the chill, the darkness, and the promise
that you remember in the years that come
when a dear lover keeps too warm and close,
would steal your memory of that night,
your longing for the freedom of the train,
your need to give an answer to its rising urgent call
until, Ulysses-like, you leave once more
to seek another world where you belong.

Albums

Photos colored, black and white, brown and tattered clippings,
letters of appointment or award, certificates, announcements,
grade reports, heaps of picture postcards from Brighton and Paris,
and all the shiny, sugary Hallmark cards for every anniversary
you kept, pasted to last forever in your albums,
quotidian joys and sorrows framed by little paste-on corners.

You loved events, occasions, parties, days fixed fast by greetings,
the mundane signposts of our lives. Recording names and dates,
you celebrated family, friends, and people you'd just met,
whose private lives and chronicles you gathered
with all the zeal of any true collector,
for no one's romance failed to have allure
and no one's troubles warranted neglect.

So — when I found you dozing on the sofa,
a month before you would be seventy-two,
your cards piled up unopened, the newspaper unclipped,
a nurse's story left untold, your albums lying dusty in their boxes,
there was no need for further diagnosis:
I knew.

The Placemat

When she died
an aide came in
to take away
her placemat
from their table,

closing the circle
where the others
huddled tighter,
her voice

an absence, a wind
they could not
hear,
her name

a mislaid word
they could not
find,
her face

a country
they might have
never visited,
her departure

just a missing
placemat
at the table.

Archaeologies at the Auberge St. Antoine

Excavated fragments from the past:
pipes and chamber pots, pieces
of plates and cups
tastefully displayed.
Bric-a-brac of lives illuminated
on shelves of glass, artifacts
turned art, memorialized as decoration
for a hotel's modern walls —
objects found beneath a city,
belongings of its old inhabitants,
displayed for visitors who see the artifacts,
if at all, as curiosities and give
no thought to their possessors.
Yet it is history informs us
and makes us who we are.
It's twenty years since mother
died, but yesterday I heard her
voice, an echo on my tongue,
felt the fragments of
her body in my face and
hands and hair, her cells
transformed in me —
forgotten and denied until
I sensed the cold outside my door
and bent and aching fingers
told of changes that must come.

Winter Soup

I am cooking the soup my mother used to make,
a good soup, thick and tangy, smelling like
cinnamon and raisins, apples and tomatoes,
spices that surface in an old and dented pot.

I can see my mother standing at the stove, stirring love
and tears into her broth with a battered spoon;
I hear the popping of bubbles
rising to the surface like my father's anger,

simmering until it came to boil and bitter to the taste.
I turn the flame to low but now my soup smells sour
till you come in and put your arms around me
and bring me back into our lives together.

At once, the fury in the soup subsides
as if the storm within the pot had passed
like some brief squall across a summer pond.
The acrid scent within the room dissolves.

My mother's soup is ready. I fill our bowls,
slice bread and fragrant cheese, and we
sit down together. No need for words.
We dip our spoons into the past and find it sweet.

II. Voices of the Poet

At times in the evenings a face
Looks at us out of the depths of a mirror;
Art should be like that mirror
Which reveals to us our own face.

Jorge Luis Borges, "Ars Poetica"

Solitude

for Emily Dickinson

Not a choice
but a necessity
I cannot live without —
retreat to the hermit's cave
where in my books
I find the nourishment
I crave to feed my body
and my soul.

Not a banning or rejection
of all I know and love
but a simple vital turn within
without which
I become an exile — alien
from who I am.

Not a cloistered separation
but a walk into a winter wood
to see the starkness of the branches
of the leafless trees against the sky,
taste the cool freshness of new snow,
smell the dryness of the ice
coating the pond
and listen to the voices
of the winds whirling inside me,
speaking to me in tongues.

Not a withdrawal but an entering
that strengthens and revives,
enabling my being in a world
I cherish but struggle to embrace —
a measuring and a narrowing
of that subtle distance
dividing each of us
from what defines us
and who we are.

Waiting Again at the Dirt Cowboy

I am sitting here in the local coffee shop
waiting for a friend. The coffee machines
roar on command, drowning out all
attempts at conversation. I, of course,
am not making an attempt to talk
above the din, because my friend is late
again. I wonder why I am so obsessive
about being on time. In my high school
days, gone now for fifty years and more,
I had a friend who was always half an hour
late. You could set your clock by her.
But I was always there waiting
at the appointed hour, could not refrain
from punctuality. Now here I am, a half
a century later, still the one on time,
still waiting. I watch the clock, order
another cappuccino, and scribble
a few more lines of a poem in progress
in my notebook. The poem is as late
in arriving as my absent friend. Maybe
my karma today just isn't in balance,
more yin than yang, perhaps. At any rate
the poem is stalled at the third stanza.
I think it needs some sex, or perhaps
a bit of angst, but neither works
for me. I mean as a topic.
I've written sad poems,
none I hope too sentimental. But joy

is the topic I like to explore and experience.
I'd like to be remembered for the things
I've loved: laughter in my house,
good food and wine on my table,
my family and my friends, including
the one who, at a full hour late,
has, I must agree, stood me up once again.

Expectation

I am the story you don't know how to find,
words spun in a centrifuge — crushed
core of colloidal cells that will not separate,
shadows on the wall of a cave.

I am the meteor that does not fall,
empty nautilus on the ocean floor,
lost gull that arcs above the foam
empty-mouthed, forgetful

of the waiting nest. I am the blankness
on the white page, the painted wall
waiting for the words,
for the writing forged from fire.

I am the nine-month pregnant woman
waiting for the child who will not come.
I am the poem hidden in the folded hand
of the arctic wind

waiting to be opened.

Eros Again

after *In the Shadow of the Wind,* Carlos Ruiz Zafon

Today in the cemetery of forgotten books,
I found a torn and faded copy of a poem
Sappho might have written,
addressed to Eros, god whose kiss
is always dipped in vinegar, whose touch,
so honeyed, arouses, but leaves behind
a longing that is infinite and unfulfilled.
The speaker of the poem summons Eros to her aid.
The one she loves is ripe and young and beautiful
but self-absorbed, and wants no love
beyond himself. The lover, desiring,
ignored, feels that she will die.
She calls the god to come to her again,
wants and needs his help
although she knows it's ever bittersweet.
Her passion makes her throat constrict, her body melt —
she fades away till just her voice remains.
The poem is a fragment and has no end.
It does not need one. Eros will not come
to the lover of the poem again,
but he will visit others, bringing rapture,
often grief. Another poet will retell the story,
for in this cemetery of forgotten books
where memories are unremembered,
but live on, poems do not die,
reborn without our calling them
so that we may write them once again.

Song

Today I read a story
of a woman paralyzed —
a stroke
had left her lame
and speechless,
her limbs and tongue
no longer hearing
the message of her brain.

She had no way to tell
her tenders
she understood
their words,
wept and raged
to be heard
and still she could not

until — against all hope
she did find speech
in song
with words articulate and strong
for she could sing
both melody and lyric
as clearly as she always had.

So when I read her story
yes, I thought,
it's when the mind
awakens
to its innermost

craving to be heard
we gain the power
to break our silences,
find the hidden source
of speech
where poems are born
and song.

Antiphonies

When the loon calls its mate
breaking the quiet surface of the lake
the sound becomes the eldritch
wail of a ghost voice
reflected from the mountains.
When the loon calls
deep within me comes a cry
no one else can hear —
call rising from a hidden place,
sanctuary of a sleeping force
that rarely wakes,
but when the loon calls
I call back.

No human hears my call
though in my ears
it choruses in full hosanna —
drums and flutes and trumpets
winging out a music
that lifts me up and up
until the sound of the loon's call
and my spirit's anthem
are fused as one.

When the loon calls
the still water
claps its hands
against the silent shore
as if it heard us both.

III. Voices of the Wild

Better than all measures
Of delightful sound,
Better than all treasures
That in books are found,
Thy skill to poet were, thou scorner of the ground!

Teach me half the gladness
That thy brain must know;
Such harmonious madness
From my lips would flow,
The world should listen then, as I am listening now.

Percy Bysshe Shelley, "Ode to a Skylark"

Ode to the Ephemeral

Painstaking in creation,
syllables entrusted
to paper's thin fragility
solidify our thoughts,
perpetuate their truth and beauty
yet fade away.

Keats was right!
Our names are writ in water.
In the face of dying
poetry becomes unequal
to the task. Our words
surviving as shadows of our selves
have no lasting shape.

But listen! What matters is today.
Across the woods
crows chatter in the trees,
sharing news of nests and food,
their communal bulletins.

The Sonnet

Once I found a sonnet within a wooded glade
formed of rocks and ripples, where foaming water welled,
its lines composed of silver notes of spring shade
and sunlight's golden laughter, peals of church-top bells.
Its rhythmic feet in summer's heat were coolness in the air
and deep beneath the winter ice, it measured out its rhyme,
so that the poem forming there was quiet as a prayer
unspoken. Its images were painted with autumn's passing time,
adorned with mossy logs, and drifts of mounting snow,
while each of its three quatrains was formed of ash or oak,
with metaphors of royal fern, or leeks or mistletoe,
its iambs banks and boulders that counted out its strokes.
But though I searched to find its couplet, its final mystery,
the sonnet had no ending. It only knew to be.

Voice of the Cricket

Yesterday a river parted
before the host of my poems
but then closed over them

drowned. When I awoke
a morning chorus
of thrush and finch

clogged my throat.
I wrote in tongues
untranslatable

crow garble, hawk croak
wren hiss,
swallow bark,

and the cricket
rubbed his legs
to sound that shrill

incessant call,
his voice on my paper
as loud as broken glass.

Indigo Bunting at the Frost Place

It isn't the blue that draws me to him,
though his is dazzling as the blue of Chartres.
No, not the blue; it is the urgency of his call,
his sense that fall is soon to come.
He's wooed his mate and raised his young,
and yet he still must sing, as if his were the voice
that summons summer's final tunes — buzz of crickets
in the grass, hum of bees in goldenrod, creep of red in maples.

It's this insistent song that punctuates the teachings
of the poet at the lectern. She speaks of form
and structure, skeleton of poems; talks of variation,
of artifice that shapes a line. The bird provides a palinode.
Written against her words, rhythm no poet ever crafted,
his poetry is woven out of air and wind and rain.
He takes me far beyond poetry, up to his tall pine
in strophe and antistrophe that turn and turn again.

Winter Wren

His song comes from a dark and secret place
of rotting logs and branches, moss and vine
and clinging lichen, woods where no sun shines —
a veil before a face.
His piercing notes cascade in rivulets of light.
I hear them rising from the forest floor,
theme that the great composers would adore,
as if he too had power to drive away the night.
I marvel that from one so very small
come mystic trills running from dawn to dark.
His cadences are perfect for a poet or a lark
for every artist feels the magic of his call.
And yet I know he sings with all his heart
to mark his turf or lure a mate, but not for art.

On Emily Dickinson's Narrow Fellow

I've seen him. He lives beneath
the granite wall that bounds my garden
and basks along the stones
when sunlight heats them to a temperature he likes.

To herpetologists he's known
as *Thamnophis Sirtalis,* serpent of the bush,
though he prefers the garden where he can dine
on earthworms, frogs and toads.

I nearly step upon his slender body. Three feet
of black and yellow stripes upon my garden steps,
forked tongue flitting in and out when I appear,
he slithers quickly back beneath the stone.

I understand that he is harmless,
has no venom, yet seeing him —
I feel a sharp and sudden
bite of fear. Remembering God's curse

on him in that first garden where we fell,
I share the chill the poet felt that day —
her "zero at the bone" — and know
her tighter breathing as my own.

Snow Geese at Bosque del Apache

Ten thousand sleeping snow geese
huddled in silent mounds,
heads down and wings
tucked in against the cold,
lie frozen on the water,
hillocks of snowy feathers
white with blue and black.
Beyond their countless shapes, gray sky,
hills looming dark, and all completely still
in clear and trembling air.

We watch a tinge of pink and yellow
wake the flock, whose murmured
morning honks begin to rise
in soft and clear crescendos,
horn players in an orchestra
finding their proper note and
trying out their sounds.

We stand in quiet ranks nearby,
shivering our shifting feet,
and wait for endless moments
to see the geese fly out to feed
until some sudden secret signal
explodes the flock together
bursting to the sky —

in clamorous cacophony
they fly row upon row
close above our heads,
filling the air with wings
and we become their rising,
our frozen bodies
pulsing with their warmth.

Lamprydae

Up from the scented grasses
in the meadow,
the quiet when the birds
have gone to nest,
among the hush of woods
and sleeping marshes,
the silent pools,
darkening streams,
into the clear night air
they lift together —
cloud of little flashing lights
that move and dance
and tell of love and death —

mercurial, winged,
transient messengers
who carry as they fly
into the night
lights fueled
by inmost driven hunger
to signal that the time
has come to mate,
that fire and heat
are part of all desire,
that burning
is the way to find relief.

Painted Trillium

A group of this year's Painted Trillium
have blossomed in a most unlikely place
where winter's done its worst to spoil the ground
and where I never thought to find them.

Behind a pile of ploughed-up weeds and dirt,
among the winter gravel and debris
they've risen up with shining pink and white,
stretching their faces to the springtime sun.

Their sudden presence in this cheerless spot
is an assertion of their need to bloom, growing
where they can — like children in a war
who play among the rubble in the streets.

Berries on the Tongue

The strawberries in my garden
ready to be picked this morning
were gone,
their bed a patch of ravaged leaves
when I went out to fetch them.

And yet their lingering fragrance
burst upon my tongue,
my lips filled
with berry scent — aromas
rich with earth and ripeness,
savory soft red flesh
sweet juices in my throat.

Filled by what I craved
I dined on berries
hoarded by my mind,
tasted by my nose —

bowl of dreams.

In Praise of Wild Leeks

Tenacious, they come up each spring
where the dirt road curves
round birch woods and dips
when it passes orange-traced tailings
of the old copper mine,
where dump trucks lumber
up the road laden with new fill
to bury the poisons in stone and sand,
and rivulets of winter's melt pollute the river below,
where woods are barred by wire fences
and windows of abandoned houses
are boarded shut, where doors hang jagged
on their frames, and forgotten gardens
bloom with piles of rusted cans,
stained mattresses, old tires,
where once, I like to think,
there were children playing,
dinners cooking, wood smoke in the air,
music flowing from lighted windows,
while in the dusk, the miners hurried home.
There in mid-April I slip around a gate
to search for leeks down a trail
into the forest that skirts the remains
of the old deserted mine,
listening to the drumming
of the grouse, insistence of the oven-bird,
arpeggios of the thrush on hillsides
purpled with spring violets.
Kneeling in shaded patches
of broad leaves, I plunge my trowel

into the rich earth, digging
my fingers down in moist chill ground
untouched by effluents
left along the river by the mine
to reap the pungent bulbs that grow so deep
I must reach up to my elbow
to pull them out.
And yet, for succulent wild leeks,
garnishes of salads and frittatas,
casseroles and soups,
I'll dig my yearly harvest
while they and I survive.

IV. In the Galleries

A poem is a picture that speaks,
A picture a silent poem.

Simonides of Keos via Plutarch

Painting the Night

on Whistler's *Nocturne: Blue and Gold – Old Battersea Bridge*

The old bridge lurks
great and dark above the Thames,
rising like a double hammer from the river,
claws clutching at the picture's frame.
Across its width plod shadow figures
who seem to make their solitary way
from one bleak world into the next.
Behind the bridge, blue-gray sky and water
can barely shine against the thrusting black,
and far below, a bank of buildings is etched
in shades of black with little golden lights
that struggle faintly to be mirrored in the water.

Without this lamp-lit line of buildings
or the delicate shower of gold in the sky
behind the bridge that might have poured
from some unseen celestial pitcher above the river
or been created by the spattering of sparks flying
from the unearthly forge that shaped the hammer,
the night would be a burden beyond bearing
for us the watchers, for the shadows crossing
high above, and for the tiny form below
upon a boat moored beneath inky pilings,
shoulders bent, head bowed
under the weight of our dark world.

Mandala: Rollins Chapel, Dartmouth College

Bent double in submission,
painting with infinite pains
and delicate precision
with rod and *chak-pur,*
in days of holy dedication,
the monks create your story,
picturing a world of perfect symmetry:
gods and fire and lotus petals
surrounding the blue thunderbolt
of Yamantaka, god who conquers death —
a miracle of balanced variation
of spirit and of matter
that is the cosmos.

Finished, your pictured prayer
reflects the mind of Buddha
and teaches that our mortal lives
are short. Your gem-like atoms
gathered in an urn
will go back to the river,
your essence born to illustrate
that earthly things must die.

As the monks mass
with chanting horns and solemn purple robes,
gathering to pour you out
beneath the water's surface,
I wait to write a palinode
against your holy text.

In fine-spun silken nets
I gather up your tiny grains
and sort your brilliant colors.
Sifting sand from liquid
I portion them anew,
greens and reds and purples,
whites and blues and yellows
I place in their containers
so you may speak again.

Reading the Reader

on Winslow Homer's *The New Novel*

No odalisque, this reclining redhead.
Pillowed on her book bag, she has gone
into the novel's world, and holds it
close within her arms lest it escape
before she has devoured it. In yellowed grass
she lies on a bed of wildflowers that seem
in full retreat before the lush ripeness of her youth,
the fullness of her hip a sensuous curve
that her concentration, her absorption in her reading
do little to belie, and that the boisterous orange
of her gown, the crimson ribbon on her shoe
sustain. Yet, posed against the slanting black-brown
of the stones of the wall behind her,
she seems quite unaware of any viewer then or now.
Content to find herself within the novel's pages,
she is walled off from anything or anyone beyond.

Tribute to a Long Love

after Pierre Bonnard's *Nude in the Bath*

Still he paints her as a young nude
though she died at sixty in 1942.
She floats again in the same tub,
her body, pink with life, in a room so full

of light and air and color
that it too floats. Here gravity
and time have ceased to be —
floor and tub, blue, red, purple,

orange tiles, her little brown dog
curled up on the floor below her —
all suspended in a collage
of dazzling paint, unanchored tub

drifting in a sea of luminosity.
Floating aloof, detached,
her buoyant body weightless,
she is lifted by her bath and looks

just as she did in 1925, the first time
he posed her bathing. Her faded years
brushed brilliant by love's constancy,
she is forever beauty's truth.

Tempests

after *Approaching Thunderstorm,* Martin Johnson Heade

Somewhere on some horizon
a storm is always building
with mounds of clouds so dark
they turn the world to ink,

and somewhere there's a rower
who's pumping towards the shore,
a sailboat tacking slowly to reach home
before the rain streaks down.

On shore may be a fisherman
sitting on a driftwood plank
with his little dog, spectators
of this tempest, in an amphitheater

still and menacing and black,
as the sky's greedy mouth
begins to close the gap of light
between clouds and sea.

Yet, in this scene it is the light
that matters, the green-gold bank,
the white sail drying on the shore,
yellow, red and orange garb of the fisherman

who waits.

Cycladic Woman

When a sculptor carved your image
he made you tall and thin, embodied
you in stone, whiter than any flesh,

gave you no ears or eyes or mouth,
your face featureless and blank,
chiseled you a mask without identity.

He stretched your torso, folded
up your arms across your pointed
breasts, moved down to carve that

triangle opened at a point between
your long and narrow legs — source of
life inside the yielding marble.

Perhaps he thought he could contain
your spirit in the faceless stone, bind up
the forces he feared were in you.

He did not know that you, deprived
of voice, of sight, of hearing, were still
invincible, your powers hidden safe within.

Elixir of Art

on Nadar's *Portrait of Sarah Bernhardt*

In this portrait she is only twenty-five.
But in Nadar's image of her, a moment held in time,
and yet not bound by it, we see into her soul
and feel the passion and the pain of a girl born
illegitimate and hidden until her mother's lover
saw the young girl's beauty, grace, and talent
that would gain her the sobriquet "Divine."
Here, in a work born in the infancy of a technology
about to transform our world, a photographer
creates a picture where art breaks down the confines
of life's years. Posed against a shadowed wall,
she is clad in a timeless drapery of ragged folds
that hide and yet suggest the fragile nakedness
and latent power they conceal. She looks out
toward events we sense but cannot see,
gazing far beyond the camera, beyond her life's great arc.

Somewhere, a Road

after Edward Hopper's *High Road*

Some roads bring us home
or where we plan to be — a house
beside a lake, apartment with a view,
family and friends who cherish us,
work that we excel in and enjoy —
or carry us to lands we've always longed to see.
Others lead to places we do not want to go,
to canyons so deep and narrow there is no light,
no air, to tunnels ending suddenly
before a wall of stone, or down a hill
to cross a river where there is no bridge,
or to a frozen lake that stops our hearts.
But there's a road through Truro
that comes from nowhere and disappears
as strangely as it came, a road that neither
beckons nor repels, a road that makes no statement,
has no dogma, no lesson to convey,
but runs between a row of wireless poles — disconnected,
yet aware of where it is, a road that rises
from a vast horizon that never seems to end
and passes just one solitary cluster of houses on its way,
a road that knows where it is going,
and how to get there, a road I choose to travel
when I can.

V. To Green Again

Inside each of us, there's continual autumn. Our leaves
fall and are blown out

over the water. A crow sits in the blackened limbs and talks
about what's gone. Then

your generosity returns: spring, moisture, intelligence, the
scent of hyacinth and rose

and cypress.

Rumi, "A Necessary Autumn Inside Each"

Santorini, 1961

Our first child curled inside me.
The kettle boiled dry
while we loved and listened to the wind's heat
caressing the flat white roof.

Once we heard the roar of motorcycles
snarling in the alley at three a.m.
as if the riders wanted passage through our room,
and island roosters crowed all night
in the neighbor's garden.
We held each other and slept
until the sun rose straight above,
touching the silent rim of the volcano's crater.

When we were hungry we ate octopus,
bread and goat cheese in a small taverna,
drank retsina and tiny cups of thick black coffee.
Weary donkeys burdened with loads
dwarfing their worn and dusty backs
struggled up the sun-scorched path below us
where lizards crept over torch-hot rocks at noon,
seeking shade in the cool, wet sand.

Beyond the ancient crusting wall
where blood-red bougainvillea clung,
the azure sea still sang
of the great fleet that sailed to Troy,
of years of longing and of pain.

We were young then —
and thought the song
of the ageless sea
was not for us.

Changing Weather

Storm clouds gather ranks above us
unwrapping darkness when the day is clear —

sliver-quick they split into sharp javelins of light.
Thunder bows the trees, unwilling worshippers,

drives choruses of birds to sudden silence.
Now blinding chords of rain make windows weep

like eyes that overflow with loss and grief
as if they mourned the passing of a sun

that's gone forever. The dogs quiver
beneath the stairs or hide between our feet;

even the cat lowers his tail, proud banner,
as if acknowledging defeat and slinks to somewhere safe.

But we, although of course we understood the day was
changing, saw mountains disappearing under mist,

heard muttering voices in branches waiting for the blast,
felt colder air replacing warm upon our skin,

rushed in too late to close our windows, shut our doors,
as if we had not known the storm would come.

That Fall

It was autumn
six years ago
when we learned
your illness had returned.

We waited.
I tended to our garden,
prepared our meals.
I walked the dog,
fed and brushed the cat.
I wrote a lecture,
refined a syllabus,
saw a student,
now and then
attempted to write
another poem.

You sat for hours
behind your shining screen
refining facts and figures
for a manuscript
you trimmed and edited.
You scanned our assets
for signs of weaknesses
that needed attention.

We both began to discard
mounds of files.
We culled the contents
of our bookshelves
and our closets,
appraised the silver,
cleaned the rugs.

We talked of daily news,
messages from friends,
our children and our grandchildren,
trips we planned to take,
shows or concerts
that we'd like to see.

Both of us lay awake at night
pretending that we slept.

That famous sword
was hanging just above us
suspended
by a single thread
so thin
so fine
so delicate
it might snap
at any moment
while we waited.

On the Day You Came Back

I rose at dawn
and went to sniff
the blueberry dew of
morning's sky
and the dogs began

to dance, catching
the wind of joy
inside the bell
of my voice,
seeing me running

to greet you
with petals of sun
in my heart,
tasting the smell
of you again

in moon-born
apple tree
branches glimmering
with welcome,
white in the dawn.

Green-up Day

How is it possible that I
am cold blue, veined blue,
woad-blue, soul-deep blue

on a day when green
is the color of morning
and a robin is cascading

song from the top of a beech?
Yesterday I tasted deep
of the bubbling nectar in my glass.

I rejoiced in the sun,
Spring Beauties in the woods,
phoebes hunting for a nest site.

Joy was a Bach cantata
playing the air around me, daffodils
and violets fortissimo in my heart.

Today, my eyes are knotted
in a blue funk,
ears garbled, tongue twisted

with words I want to say to you,
but can't. Here I am
waiting — for my mind to green again.

Nankang Morning

Five o'clock a.m.
In silence, we watch for birds
along a muddy rice field.
Four egrets bend slender necks,
breakfasting on frogs and crabs.
They do not see us.

Above, an eagle soars,
his screams against the quiet
a reminder
of how desperately
twice we've battled death.

He disappears. Song teases us,
hidden in the crowded brush.
We search,
can almost touch the melody
it is so close.
We cannot find the singer,
do not mind —

we are together still
this Nankang morning;
discovery does not matter.
Time's feathers hold their breath for us.
Hope is just a leaf,
a branch away.

Icarus: Early Morning

I wake abruptly as another
morning comes between us in our bed
where you lie snoring in spurts and honks,
incessant rumble in my ears,
so that I am half conscious — enough to long
to escape from your rude trumpeting,
our aging bodies. I pillow
my head and fall asleep again
and dream I have feathers
carrying me so high that the earth
swims below in an ocean of stars
where being alone is all there is and all
I want and I am flying higher, fleeing
towards the sun's bright core when suddenly
my feathers start to drift away and I am falling
down and down into a rumpled sea
of sheets, and I wake again to silence
and reach over to find our bed empty
and I get up and look out the window to see
you and the dog climbing through timothy grass
below the house we built where we are growing old
together. I have come home.

Winter

1.

Under the ice in the pond
deep, a heart
frozen.

Fields of grasses
caught by drifts —
no comfort.

Hunger
leaves its footprints
in the snow.

In naked trees
arms hold emptiness,
cry out,

All roads go where they will —
miles of cold,
no rest.

2.

Who can teach the birds
that stay the why
of suffering

or show wet eyes
the how
of sadness?

In the mud under the pond,
green frogs wait
for spring.

Winter Midnight in the Village

Before the plows can come to spoil it all,
we don our skis, put on our warmest gloves,
collect the dogs, and make our way along the empty streets.

Time hangs suspended. The dogs are strangely still.
The old, historic houses, fenced and fortified
by piled up drifts of new blown snow,

stand alert and watching as we go softly by,
their clapboard sides, their aged, hoary,
weathered faces luminescent in the quiet cold.

A few lights flicker in communion from the shuttered
windows as we glide behind the village school; by the
steepled church, we think we hear the sounds of voices

in the darkened hall. The muted street lights veiled
by falling snow, the giant beeches decked in
winter white, the narrow snow-bound lanes

conspire together to form their world anew,
as if they were a council of wise New England elders
holding a midnight meeting to take their village back.

Snow Light

As a full moon shines on pure white snow
in coldest darkest winter,
earth glows with such a pale, blue light
it turns our woods into a forest
of black-gray trees of every shape
that lie across the shining ground
and call us from the house.

More than mere shadows,
these trees are born of some unearthly seed
which ripens only now,
a mystic coupling of light and snow
that in the warmth of snow light
produces ghostly fingers
that touch the snow
and waken mystery.

When snow light beckons
with its transfiguring glow,
a promise emanates
for some few nights
and makes us kings and shepherds
who trust in prophecies,
believing in this harbinger
of better days to come.

VI. LOSING

We stand
looking at the ruin of our garden
in the early dark of November, hearing crows
go over while the first snow shines coldly
everywhere. Grief makes the heart
apparent as much as sudden happiness can.

Jack Gilbert, "Harm and Boon in the Meetings"

Losing

The yellow eye of a bright blue
forget-me-not in my garden
looked up at me today,
reproaching me for absent-mindedness.
I planted it last year and I'd forgotten
where it lay. That look is haunting me.
Yesterday I lost my iPod, the day
before, some pills I thought
were safely stored.
And last week a book
I knew I'd bought and put upon a shelf
vanished. Words too are so much harder
to retrieve. I know I had them,
but they no longer
come on cue, waiting till I think
they're really gone and then
emerging. And yet forgetfulness
is just a symptom. A while ago
I lost another dog
to old age and disease,
a timid Springer Spaniel
who barked at bikes and boxes
but no one ever feared.
That isn't all. I've lost a younger brother
and a much beloved friend.
That losing comes with loving
is, I know, a given.
Still, loving is a habit
that I can not break — a bird
whose nest is plundered
every year, I build again
in the same fragile place.

Looking Back

We long to repossess our lives' epiphanies,
to recreate our first encounter
with Chartre's brilliant blue,
stand again beneath the Parthenon,
or climb Mt. Washington
on a perfect day,
but looking back is dangerous,
its joys paired with pain:
a long, last walk in a house
we loved and had to leave,
footsteps echoing through silent, empty rooms,
a laugh that sounds like someone
we held dear, now gone.
So Lot's wife, looking back, was turned to salt.

The Pillow

She used to wish she had a nickel
for every argument they had
about the pillow and where
it should be placed, on his side
or on hers. The quarrel was absurd.
It was the shabbiest and most stained
of pillows, its surface marred
by random moles and veins that
rise up when a pillow gets too old
and all its feathers start to molt
and stick together. It smelled the way
some dreams do, made of sweat and salt
and fog. Still, they fought to have it:
for all its flaws, it had the soft allure
of something known and trusted,
like a tattered teddy bear you've kept in secret,
or an old friend who knows just who you are.
But when he went away with a new lover
and left the pillow lying on their bed, she didn't
want it anymore: their argument was dead.

Near-Drowning off Tulum

Blue-green water swells and roils around my body,
slaps my face, fogs my mask. World of calm and silence
gone. The battered fishing boat, my life-preserver,
its Mayan captain, who dropped us into a quiet sea, gone.
The reef, its coral branches, starfish, seaweed,
silver, blue, and yellow fish in the garden below me
gone. Some giant squid or pterodactyl has snatched
the others. Gone. I am alone, as if I have fallen
from an ocean liner far from land. I cannot see its smoke
or hear its engine. No warning blasts, no life-boat.
Gone. Just the rough beating of the angry sea
against my mask, whiteness of my water-withered
hands, my webbed feet. On the beach, somewhere
on another planet, a few bikini-clad oiled bodies
entice the morning sun, palm trees bend in worship
of the wind, children flirt with the mounting waves,
ride them with rodeo daring, whooping, tumbling.
In foam and sand they are tossed to land.
Near the shore, pelicans and terns troll for fish.
I flail, kick, swim towards a land I can no longer see.
Gone. Something cold touches me. My body stiffens.
A shark, sting-ray, Man of War?
Another bump. A firm hand. Our guide smiles at me.
I see the others. Terror and the angry waves
gone. I am safe again — for now.

At the Bridge

I like to follow the slow purl of our great river,
its gathering together for the big
drop downstream where the dam holds most of it back.

Upriver where I live, the water is dark and deep
and hides a current cold in its depths that can catch
a swimmer and keep him down. I remember

that hot July morning when I was walking
across the new bridge that links two states —
how I found some bathing trunks on the bridge

and wondered where their owner might be. Later
that day I heard about the student who had joined
a group in the traditional nude midnight swim

across the river at its widest section. The trunks
were his, but when the others reached the bank
and climbed up on the rocks, he was not there,

nor on the other bank where they'd begun.
They called for help, and people came,
put out boats and sent down divers

into the river's belly, hunting between
the two shores, while the boats above them
rose and fell to the breathing of the water.

After hours of searching they found the boy
on the bottom, curled body white in the river weeds,
rocked by the slow purl of the river as if he were asleep.

Elegy for a Good Man

In Memoriam Donald Sheehan, 1940-2010

It was his bright blue eyes that captivated
before you ever saw the long white beard,
the modest gingham shirt and sandaled feet,
or heard the dulcet tones of a voice
so gentle that it seemed more like
prayer and very often was —
his was a spiritual and a simple world.
When his students read their poems to him
his first response when they had finished
was always one word —"beautiful,"
and by the magic of that pure spoken word,
the poems were, for he understood the hearts
of poets more than anyone I've ever known,
heard each novice work with such an open mind
that he could find the essence in the core
of someone's poem and make it sing for its creator,
no matter how unpolished it might be.
He knew the best of bards of every age
and hosted the most successful poets
of our time at annual Frost Place Festivals,
but still he asked them to remember they were there
as colleagues among all the writers who attended,
despite awards and accolades they'd garnered,
and when each festival commenced,
he spoke of love and generosity, of the vital need
to find the unique beauty in another's work,
to value it as if it were our own — his legacy for us.

Raven Call

I woke this morning to a heavy mist
that hid the hills beyond our meadow,
concealing all the woods,

but shortly rose, unveiling as it went
vermillion flame and brilliant golden-orange
of autumn leaves. The woods,

bereft of spring and summer birds,
still seemed to want to claim an immortality
in boldest speechless oratory,

as if such colors would stay forever,
branches splashed indelibly,
leaves fixed in all their splendor,

so that the falling of the leaves,
mornings dark and cold with frost,
evenings long and black and bleak

would never come. Then, a solitary raven,
piercing the solemn stillness of the morning,
called through a woods still shimmering

with shifting panes of multicolored light
and broke the morning's spell,
reminding me.

Phoebes in May

All spring they called
for hours while I was sowing
summer in the ground:
plants for bees and butterflies.
Swift flying astronauts,
they flitted above the meadow
among the beech and birch,
and darted low into the lilacs.
They chanted their mantic song
as they winged from eave to eave,
searching for the perfect place to build their nest.
When May arrived, I discovered that they
were nesting in our woodshed's peak
where the rafters rise church-like
and where above the roof
the weathervane rings out squeaky tunes,
metronome of change turned by sudden winds.
I found the nest on a dark rafter
where safety should have dwelled.
Next day some plotting predator
broke down the nest and stole
its future brood. On the shed floor, I gathered
fragile shells of possibility unborn.
And as I did the phoebes called and called.

Lost Children

You see them on the streets of every city.
They shine your shoes or try to sell you beads;
they barter woven goods or dirty pictures
and pick your pocket if they have the chance.
They sell their bodies to anyone who pays
or do the work that no one else will do,
trade all they have to get a piece of pizza,
survive in packs or travel all alone.
They sleep in tunnels or in empty boxes,
find pleasure shooting up or sniffing glue.

They carry no address or treasured pictures,
no letters that remind them they are loved.
For them no baths, clean clothes, or cherished playthings,
no shelter from ones who'll do them wrong;
for them, no tickets to a better passage,
no happy endings when the engine stops;
for them, the journeys end in their beginnings;
for them, there is no train at all.

Building Walls

Before I built a wall I'd ask to know
What I was walling in or walling out,
and to whom I was like to give offense.

Robert Frost, "Mending Wall"

Perhaps the poet knew
that other walls would come
in later times,
requiring more than elves
to knock them down.

Built at enormous cost of lives
and resources, walls isolate us,
divide us, rich from poor, black from white,
German from German, Arab from Jew,
Mexican from North American
and friends from friends,
families from families.

Built, their makers say, to keep us safe
these walls do the just the opposite —
wooden, rock, cement, iron, barbed wire
stretching for miles between us,
cancers on the landscape,
all of us on either side
while they still stand,
their prisoners.

Animas Canyon

From an arid land of heat
the Canyon of the Spirits called us in,
birds of the forest chorusing in song
that drew us there to find them.
We passed the open gate
and walked along the wooded road,
reveling in the coolness and the peace.

But then, a silent shadow
we had not felt or seen
fused into human shape,
stepped into our path,
shouted and blocked our way —
a uniformed and armed militia man
whose task it was to keep the canyon safe
against the hostile world outside.

Cursing us, the canyon guardian
raised a rifle so that we fled in fear,
and as we went, he closed and locked
the iron gate that shut the road at night —
Lucifer protecting his fallen paradise.

The Tears of Horses

When Achilles' horses wept
to mourn his comrade's death,
the churning world grew quiet —

you could hear the sound of
teardrops raining slowly down
across the war-worn globe,

could feel the pain of soldiers
wounded in the field, could touch
the hopes of fathers and of wives

in waiting for the footsteps
that would never sound again,
could taste the sweetness drying

on children's hopeful lips,
could see the breath
of mothers making evening meals

their sons would never eat,
could gather up in weeping horses' tears
whole oceans full of misery and loss.

Remnants

based on a photo from Srebrenica

I see your tented, black-robed
figures bent in quiet agony,
your hands and shrouded faces
etched by waiting and despair.
You search to find the remnants
of your husbands and your sons
in pictures of their clothing
dug from a common grave,
photographed and itemized,
the album of your dead.

I watch as you make your search
in silence for your men,
turning through the pages,
looking for a sign
amidst the soiled and empty shirts,
the torn and tattered trousers
and ragged muddy socks,
the twisted hats and threadbare coats
and worn and broken shoes,

watch pale and trembling hands
reach out as if you felt
these cold and silent images
grow warm —
as if your men were living still
and you could cook their meals,
wash their shirts, mend their
socks and trousers.

Though you do not speak or weep
before you close the album,
I hear your voiceless cry.

They Go On

I did not see the hawk come down today,
silent raptor diving through the air
to strike its target among the feeding chickadees

and titmice. No, I did not see or hear the hawk,
but the soft gray feathers scattered on the ground
told of the desperate struggle — the will to live,

a battle lost, another hungry victim
taken to be eaten. When I looked
at those sad feathers and at the flock of birds

back gathering food around the vestiges of death,
I thought of how survivors of a suicide attack go on
day after day shopping again at the local market

where the bomber struck, for they must eat,
birds returning to their winter feeder
to gather seeds again when the hawk has flown,

though not for good.

A Picture from Beslan

A woman kneels beside a blanket
on the ground, beside a little girl,

a child who lies upon the grass
as if asleep. The woman bends above

the girl as if she's come to tuck her in,
turn off her light, and say goodnight.

But the figure on the blanket does not move,
and the grass is crowded with the bodies

of her friends, children who shared the horror —
hunger, thirst, and fear, bullets, bombs, and fire.

In the photograph, the woman seems suspended,
face untouched by recognition and by grief

as if she has been captured in that second before sorrow:
time when hope and possibility still live.

Falling Snow

to Orhan Pamuk

I lay aside your book to war with the frozen earth,
digging for dahlia bulbs I left beneath the ground
too long, pushing my trowel hard against the frost
and rocks of tough New England soil,
and think I smell a warm and spicy odor,
tenacious roots of all the hum and buzz
of summer's bounteous blossoming,
redolent aroma of crimson Bee Balm
red as the flag of Istanbul, as the Bokaras
in those myriad shops of rugs that populate the streets
of your far off Istanbul. I imagine that I drink again
translucent cups of rich and pungent tea, hear the evening
call of the muezzin, stand again beneath the breathless dome
of Hagia Sophia, see the beauty and the squalor
of the city streets, the air of seedy disrepair
amidst the glorious monuments of bygone grandeur.

But then, a sudden snow squall fills the air
around my garden and sends me back inside
to find your book, and I am in a remote Turkish city
cold and filled with deepening snow banks,
where revolutionaries fail to throw away the past
and girls are killed for honor's sake —
a buried world of endless falling snow.

Beacon Wood, Hampshire

for Geoffrey Dashwood

Today no fires gleam from Beacon Wood
beyond the giant oaks above the valley.
Here a sculptor does his work,
plying a craft older than Greece itself,
shaping forms in wire and clay,
readying them for plaster and for wax,
his molds for casting bronze — images
not gods or heroes,
but birds of every size and every feather —
warblers, finches, herons, owls, and hawks.
Planted in his garden and his shop,
their forms are rooted, beyond change.

Once there were great stone towers
on his hill beneath the ancient oaks,
towers crowned with beacons
to give warning of the Spanish fleet
like the beacon fires that reached
from far-off Troy to Agamemnon's palace
across the wine-dark sea
to shine among the stone-worn hills
of Argos, beacons whose lights bore the word
that Troy had fallen, but brought no peace
for the great warriors who fought there.

Here we can see the broad grey-silver channel
where the mighty fleet was driven off,
and stand beneath the timeless oaks
that frame the sculptor's art —
here in this place where art and nature
coexist in peace, we can forget for a brief time
fires burning all around our world,
conflagrations that will not go out.

VII. Lessons

I pursue ephemeral joy,
but in calm I approach old age
and the time appointed.
Our destinities are different,
but all of us will die.

Pindar, "Isthmian 7"
(translation by the author)

Lesson on the Meaning of Life

When too many cold gray days in a row,
rank after rank of them
march over the snow-topped mountains

I ponder how to gather light again,
how to drive away the chill
that pulses in my heart —

fundamental questions
made urgent by the empty
woods still waiting to be full

of the certainty of bird song.
The questions —
how to be patient, to accept what

I can't change, problems as daunting
as clipping the claws on the cat,
proud, stubborn creature

whose long ginger fur collects
sunlight as if it belongs to him,
but when it comes to claws

he bites and struggles,
unmoved even by the beatitudes
of warmth or food or stroking.

No questions for him —
he has all the answers
he needs.

Letter to a Lover

Don't say you love me in nearly shouted oaths —
endearment in hyperbole diminishes us both.
No slappity-slap of syllables when we turn off the light —
a soft caress of whispered balm is always right.

You make of love a battle, are ever on attack,
and the result, my dear, just puts me on the rack,
I don't contest your passion; it's simply very loud.
Please take a vow of silence, even in a crowd.

I like the tiny pricking of a promise in my ears,
find erotic pleasure in words that no one hears,
so if you wish to woo me, and you seem to think you do,
don't write your love in majuscule; send me a billet-doux.

You'll find a quiet letter
works so much better.

Through Windows

Journeying to somewhere we think we need to go
we look in lighted windows on our way,
catch glimpses of the private worlds inside
that seem to shine with luminescent gold
transforming ordinary rooms
to things so perfect and unreachable
our looking brings us emptiness and pain.

Inside may be a woman writing at a desk,
a couple sitting at their evening meal,
their table glowing in the candle light,
their crystal glasses shimmering red with wine,
perhaps an upstairs room alert with eager waiting,
an antique bed with covers folded down
and slippers placed for someone yet to come.

And in the dark, desire overwhelms us
to take possession of the lives we see,
to penetrate the private worlds of strangers
and hold them frozen in their fleeting moment,
as if they held the key to what eludes us,
means to grasp what always lies beyond us,
revealed and disappearing in seconds as we pass.

A Lesson from Ovid

Oil spills are spreading, their poison
eating through our waters, their greedy fingers
reaching to devour the marshes, the inlets,
deltas, beaches; to soak the feathers
of the gannet, tern, pelican, egret, snowy plover
till they are flightless, and suffocate shrimp,
crabs, menhaden, snappers, groupers.
But still we drill, our need for oil
unquenchable, our comfort, our mobility
continually famished. It is as if our very blood
were oil and when a rig explodes and spills,
we birth a plague that cannot be contained,
profaning our own "holy places" as once,
the poet says, Eyrsichthon, King of Thessaly did,
who dared to topple an ancient sacred oak of Ceres,
his sacrilege repaid by all-consuming famine
that filled him, planting a hunger in him
he could not sate, his gaping crop
forever emptying and filling, and when his wealth
was gone he even sold his daughter to buy food
that could not satisfy the gnawing in his gut,
until at last to pacify the raging hunger
in his belly's hollow cavern, he fed upon himself.

The Key to It All

Try to remember where you last had the key.
Look for it in the ashes of yesterday's fire.
Stir charred remnants of oak or birch,
last breaths of living wood. Break apart
the pieces and grind them to dust.
Empty all the flowerpots, un-dig your garden,
re-walk all the trails that circle
through the woods. Pick up every stone
and log and rummage through the dirt.
Turn all the seams of your coats and pants and jackets
inside out. Dump the contents of your purse
onto the floor. Sort through the pens
and crumpled lists of shopping
done at least a year ago, receipts, lipstick
and stuck-together cough drops.
Write all your relatives and friends.
Ask them if they have seen it.
Keep looking. Don't give up the hunt.
Search the pockets of your imagination
where in some soft corner
full of balls of dust and cobwebs
a little golden key may hide.
Keep up the search through days
and weeks and years until
when you are old and weary
you have forgotten why you're looking,
or realize you never had the key
and didn't really need it.

Geometries

Now in my mid-seventies
I always have to remind myself
to keep to the left
when I drive in Great Britain,
especially in roundabouts.
It's so easy to forget where I am
and to enter the right lane by mistake.
I have to confess, though, that
I like the structure and the concept
of going round about.
In school I liked geometry's
exploration of forms and shapes
of many kinds of curves and arcs.
They were so much more appealing
than triangles and squares
and much more sensuous
than the predictable straightness of the line.
I remember being in a line
in Hanover, New Hampshire
where some other grey-haired
people in the queue
were very anxious about the way
the line curved. They worried
about latecomers not finding
the line's end and cutting in.
They were afraid if that happened
they would not get their favorite seat.
Not even the fact the line was actually
quite short
could stifle their fears. The line insisted

on its inner right to be a circle,
its own essential crookedness,
and that was just intolerable
to these ticket holders. Still, they
were going to an opera and should
have known random twists and turns
must be expected in the course
of art and life — even when one is
just standing still and waiting.

On the Train to Cambridge

Out our window a green wind
dances silver-toed
over field on field of bending grass.

High above us, a hawk wind-hovers
as if his pulsing wings
could hold him there forever.

We rush past waiting stations
whose painted names are speed-blurred
so that we are off our map,

reminder of how easily we lose location,
how fast our lives fly by,
how years reduce to moments,

our parents dead before we really knew them,
our children bearing children
almost before we saw that they were grown,

chapters of our story moving to conclusions
while we are writing introductions.
Like our speeding train, we seldom stop

to hang suspended like the Sparrow Hawk,
who watches for a rustle in the grass,
then dives to grasp it for his own.

Vermont Pastoral

No shepherds here,
no fecund goats,
no pails of brimming milk
or love-struck simple lads,
no piping melodies
that echo in refrain,
no prizes for the song
that seems the best,
no carven cups
of fresh-cut wood
that picture worlds
beyond the rustic peace,
no promises of
golden times to come —
Arcadia has vanished
as it must.

But here are woods
with old stone walls
and birdsong rising up,
long shaded paths
with trailing vines,
and meadows full
of tall sweet grass
beset by clumps of vetch,
a romp of dogs,
and chimney swifts
who chatter up above,

the joyful notes
of children playing
in the field —
the summer time
of pastoral,
idyllic and ephemeral:
poetry to help us
bear the dark.

Philosophy

Socrates, my life is unexamined,
directed by some force beyond
my agency, a windless weathervane.

Just when I think my sextant's holding
true, I hit a valley or a mountain
that I did not see, crash on the rocks

of accident, as if some new-discovered
element had drawn the needle of
my compass to an unknown direction

designed by some elusive atom
whose electron is chaotic,
its path uncertainty.

I've tried to understand
the movement of my soul,
to plot its course, to question

its intentions, unveil its deepest
thoughts and plumb its voyage.
Instead, the map I have has latitudes

and longitudes outside of any
globe I know — it puts the stars
beneath the ground,

shows snowstorms in July,
a field of daffodils in winter,
train tracks going nowhere in the sky.

And so, I do not try to comprehend
parchments with letters I
cannot read, refuse to look

for hidden meanings in
those random pages that chronicle
my life as one worth living.

In place of you, I take the Hermit
Thrush as my philosopher,
sage bird who teaches me
with melody transcending thought.

Touchstone

At the side of a long road
a gray-haired woman passes
on her way to somewhere
whose name she does not know.

Within her hands she holds
a gold and silver cup —
inside, a shining stone
she found inside a rainbow.

She sings a little song
into the cup to stir the stone
and make it glow — it rotates
slowly, rises and subsides.

Touching the stone will bring
her youth and beauty,
a figure slim and firm,
perhaps a handsome prince.

She knows the power of
the stone and loves to see
it turn, but will not
reach inside to loose its force,

for youth and beauty
and romance are not
what she desires —
she is content

to keep the stone
she does not touch,
and be a gray-haired woman
on any road she goes.

Curriculum Vitae at Seventy-Four

Did I dream when we were young
and full of hope, we'd always dance all night,
work all day without a sign of weariness?

Our yesterdays have vanished
as quickly as the breath of summer
I felt this morning brush my lips as I awoke.

What we have done in all our years
is printed on pages
soon forgotten like dusty books
aging on shelves that no one ever visits.

But in early dew to have traced the tracks
of the fox's journey through the meadow,
pattern of turkeys' passage in the snow,
to have seen a shower of Perseids,

to have watched the glow of Northern Lights,
have sat beneath the reddening maple tree
beside the pond, listening to the silence
of leaves floating on its surface,

to have watched the growing
of our children's children,
and to have held each other through times of
pain and darkness

will have been enough.

About the Author

Phyllis Beck Katz's poems have appeared in many journals including *The Connecticut River Review, The New England Anthology, Ekphrasis, Bloodroot Literary Magazine,* and *The Salon.* She received her B.A. in English from Wellesley College, her M.A. in Greek from UCLA, and her Ph.D. in Classics from Columbia University. She taught English and Classics at The University of Illinois, City University of New York, SUNY Purchase, the College of New Rochelle, and Miss Porter's School. Since 1993 she has taught at Darmouth College, offering undergraduate classes in Classics as well as Women's and Gender Studies. She has also taught classes in poetry, cultural studies, and gender issues as part of the Master of Arts in Liberal Studies program. She and her husband, Arnold, have four children and eight grandchildren. She has traveled extensively and enjoys cooking, biking, hiking, and bird-watching.

www.PhyllisBeckKatz.com

This book is set in Garamond Premier Pro, which had its genesis in 1988 when type-designer Robert Slimbach visited the Plantin-Moretus Museum in Antwerp, Belgium, to study its collection of Claude Garamond's metal punches and typefaces. During the mid-fifteen hundreds, Garamond—a Parisian punch-cutter—produced a refined array of book types that combined an unprecedented degree of balance and elegance, for centuries standing as the pinnacle of beauty and practicality in type-founding. Slimbach has created an entirely new interpretation based on Garamond's designs and on comparable italics cut by Robert Granjon, Garamond's contemporary.

To order additional copies of this book
or other Antrim House titles, contact the publisher at

Antrim House
21 Goodrich Rd., Simsbury, CT 06070
860.217.0023, AntrimHouse@comcast.net
or the house website (www.AntrimHouseBooks.com).

•

On the house website
are sample poems, upcoming events,
and a "seminar room" featuring supplemental biography,
notes, images, poems, reviews, and
writing suggestions.